Brain Box
WOW!
Cool Kid
deep thinking
out of this world
CW01583223
?
hidden treasure
WOW!
teacher's pet
so true...
FAB!
Super Star
Know it all!
!
high flyer
time for tea !
!
Maths Whizz
No. 1
Hidden Treasure
out of this world
hard cheese
?
deep thinking
Know it all!
Star pupil
HELP!
Fab at Fractions
GREAT AT GRAPHS
? Huh
easy peasy
Great idea!
TOP MARKS
10 out of 10
rocket science
lost the plot
FAB!
time for tea !
?
Fab at Fractions
easy peasy
No. 1
WELL HARD
10 out of 10
TOP MARKS
time for maths
out of this world
puzzled?
out of this world
lost the plot
deep thinking
Maths Whizz
GREAT AT GRAPHS
HELP!
rocket science
over the moon
high flyer
?
FAB!
Maths Whizz
TOP MARKS
time for maths
Hidden Treasure
No. 1
% Mega at = Maths +
out of this world
Maths Whizz
easy peasy
time for tea!
?
hard cheese
100% maths
TOP MARKS
!
FAB!
WELL HARD
? Huh
high flyer
now we're moving
well done!
over the moon
10 out of 10
MEGA
% Mega at Maths +
out of this world

Contents

About this book

Mega Counting 3–5 offers lots of practice in counting skills as described in the Curriculum Guidance for the Foundation Stage. The book reflects the content of the National Curriculum in England and Wales and the National Guidelines for Scotland.

In this book, children will learn to count from zero to twenty, and to:

1. say the names of the numbers;

2. point to pictures (objects) as they are counted;

3. understand that we say one number for each object counted;

4. recognise and write the numbers;

5. match numbers to pictures;

6. make simple calculations, e.g. add more objects to make a given number (addition), share objects equally (division).

The book is aimed at children aged 3 to 5, so the levels of the exercises are progressively more difficult, for example, there are many more calculations in the second half of the book. The content begins at Nursery level and moves up to Reception level. We recommend that your child works through the book in the given order. If he or she starts to struggle or gets bored with any of the pages, skip these questions and return to them on another day when your child is feeling more positive and responsive. Repetition and practice will help build skills and confidence.

Your child can add the 100 fun stickers to the pages of the book as rewards for his or her efforts or use them to decorate pencil cases, posters or other items.

How to... pages contain useful parent notes.

Checklist to record your child's achievements.

How to help your child

Choose a time when your child is alert and eager to learn. Read aloud and point to the instructions on each page. These are written using a simple vocabulary for the age group, but you may also need to explain more fully what your child is being asked to do. Make sure your child can hold a pencil correctly and let your child decide how long he or she wants to work on the book.

Always give lots of encouragement and praise for effort and enjoy the book together.

Learn to write the number 0

Zero is a special number.

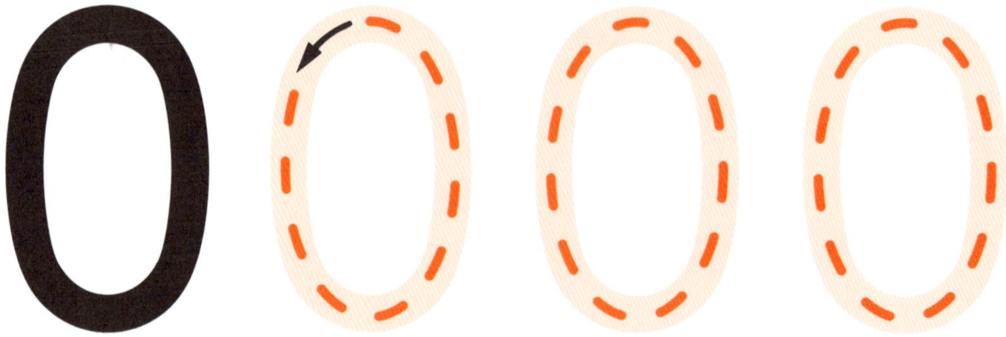

Start at the black arrow and follow the red lines.
Try to keep inside the red shadow.

Can you count any rabbits in the garden?

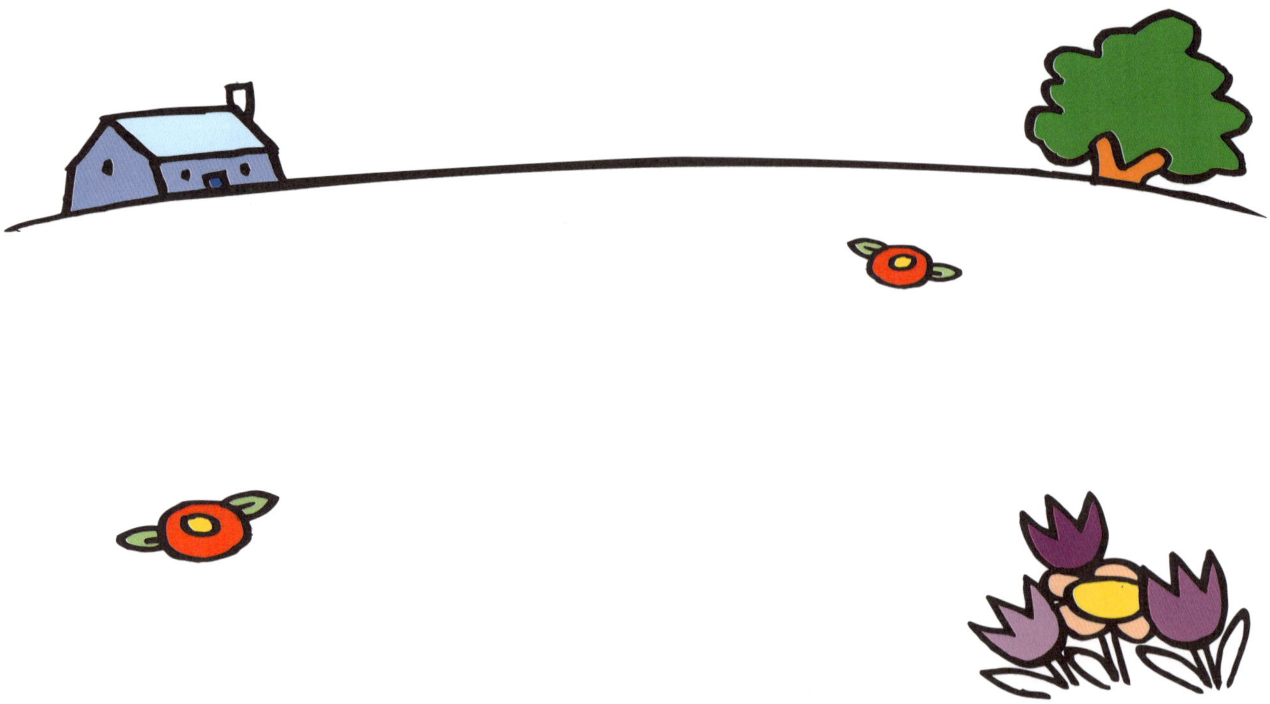

Can you see any dogs in the kennel?
There are no dogs.

Count I

Look at the tree.
Can you count any birds in the tree?
No, there is nothing in the tree.

Look at this tree.
Can you count any birds now? Yes, there is one bird in the tree.

10

Write 1, count 1

Follow the lines to write the number one.

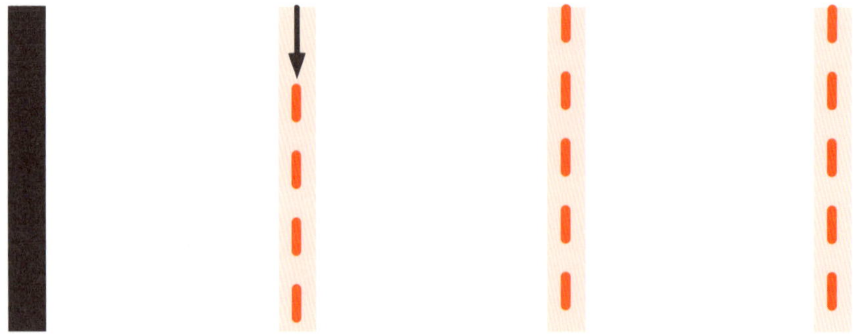

Count one rabbit.

Can you count any dogs in the garden?
Colour the dog.

Can you see one cat hiding behind the kennel?

Learn to write the number 2

Follow the lines to write the number two.

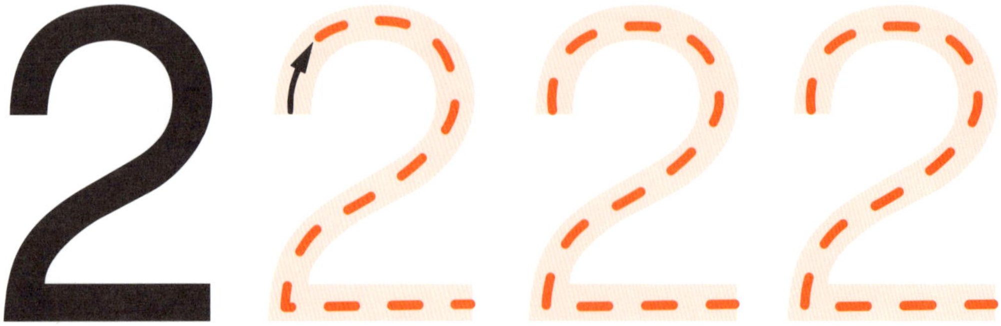

Count two planes.

Count two dogs.
Colour two bones.

Count to 3

How many birds in the tree?
Two. There are two birds in the tree.

Count the birds in this tree. How many are there?
There are three birds in the tree.

Learn to write the number 3

Follow the lines to write the number three.

3

Count three spiders.

Write 3, count to 3

Count three pieces of cheese.
Colour three mice.

How to count

Counting isn't just about reciting the numbers 1 to 10 by heart. A well-trained parrot is able to do this, but a parrot has no real understanding of what the numbers actually mean.

To aid your child's understanding of counting and numbers, you can:

- **point to each picture (or object) as it is counted on the page;**
- **explain that we say one number for each picture counted;**
- **talk about the shapes of the numbers as they are written.**

Ring the numbers that match the pictures.

0 1

0 1

0 1

0 1

Recognise numerals

Ring the numbers that match the pictures.

0 1 2

0 1 2

0 1 2

0 1 2

Ring the numbers that match the pictures.

0 1 2 3

0 1 2 3

0 1 2 3

0 1 2 3

22

Count to 3, order numbers

Draw three candles on the cake.

Say the truck numbers in order.
Write the numbers on the trucks.

Learn to write the number 4

Follow the lines to write the number four.

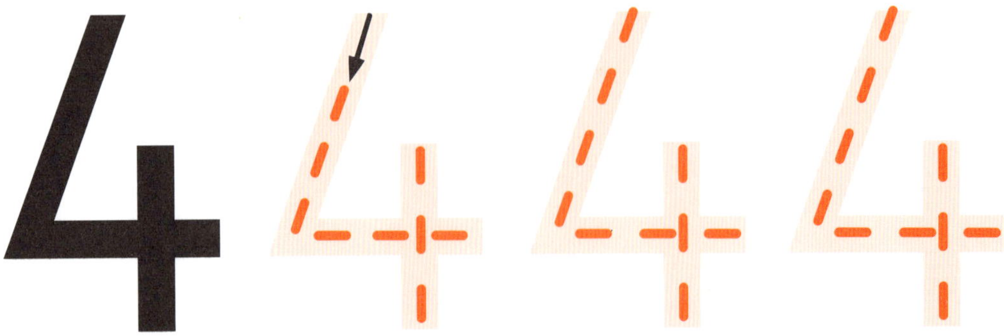

Count four legs.

Count four chairs.
Colour four plates.

Count to 5

How many birds in the tree?
Count four birds.

How many birds now?
Are there five?

Learn to write the number 5

Follow the lines to write the number five.

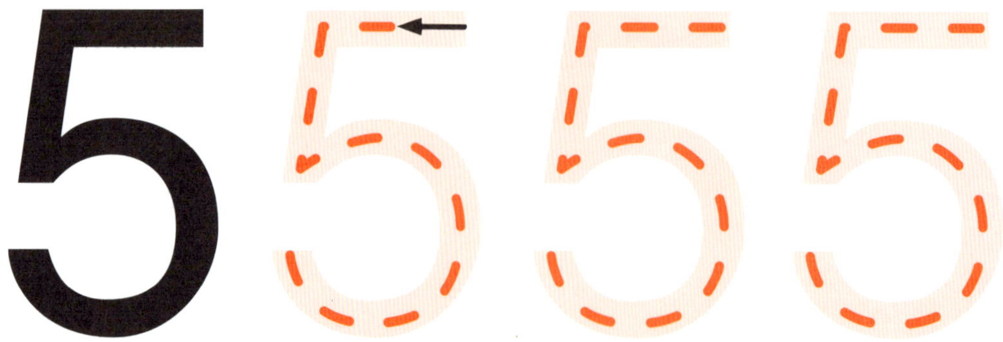

Count five petals.

Count to 5

Here are five flowers. Count them.
Colour five plant-pots.

Recognise numerals

Ring the numbers that match the pictures.

0 1 2 3 4

0 1 2 3 4

0 1 2 3 4

0 1 2 3 4

Ring the numbers that match the pictures.

0 1 2 3 4 5

0 1 2 3 4 5

0 1 2 3 4 5

0 1 2 3 4 5

32 Count to 5, write numerals

Here are five monkeys.
Count and colour them.

Here are five snails.
Write the numbers on their shells.

Order numbers, count to 5

Say the hat numbers in order.
Write the numbers on the hats.

Count the spots on the dice.
Write the numbers.

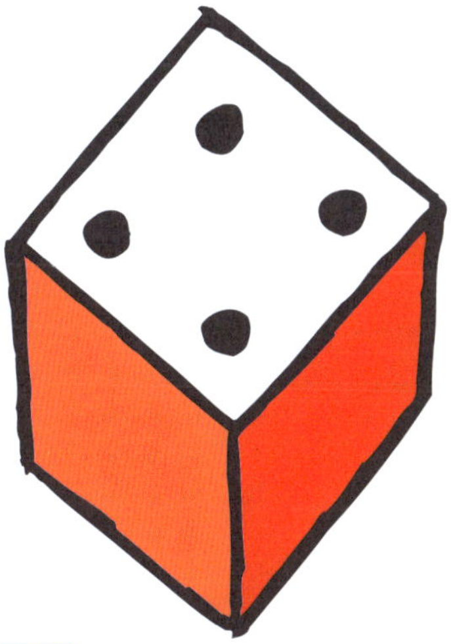

☐ **spots**

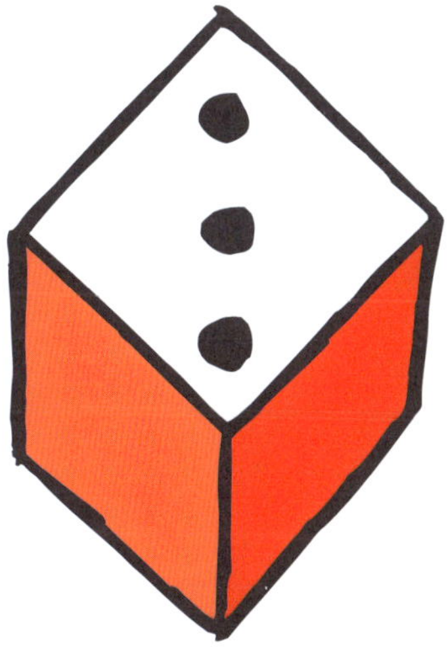

☐ **spots**

☐ **spots**

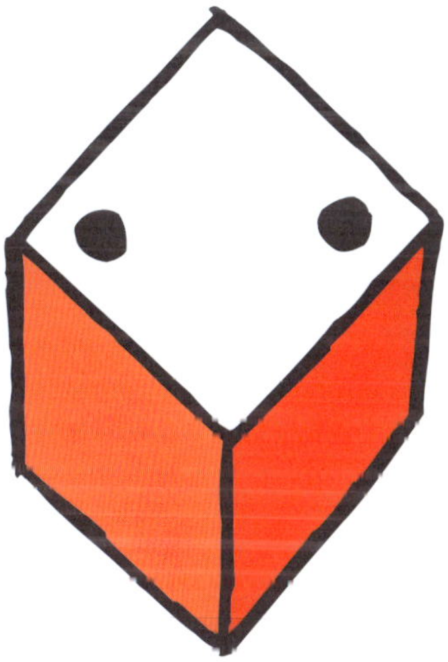

☐ **spots**

Count the bananas.
Write the numbers.

How many? ☐

How many? ☐

How many? ☐

How many? ☐

Draw some more fruit to match each number.

3 pears

5 apples

2 oranges

4 plums

Recognise numerals

Ring the numbers that match the pictures.

0 1 2 3 4

0 1 2 3 4

0 1 2 3 4

0 1 2 3 4

Ring the numbers that match the pictures.

0 1 2 3 4 5

0 1 2 3 4 5

0 1 2 3 4 5

0 1 2 3 4 5

Recognise numerals

Draw lines to join the pictures to the numbers.

0

1

3

Draw lines to join the pictures to the numbers.

2

5

3

Order numbers, count to 5

Join the dots. Start at zero.
Colour the tree.

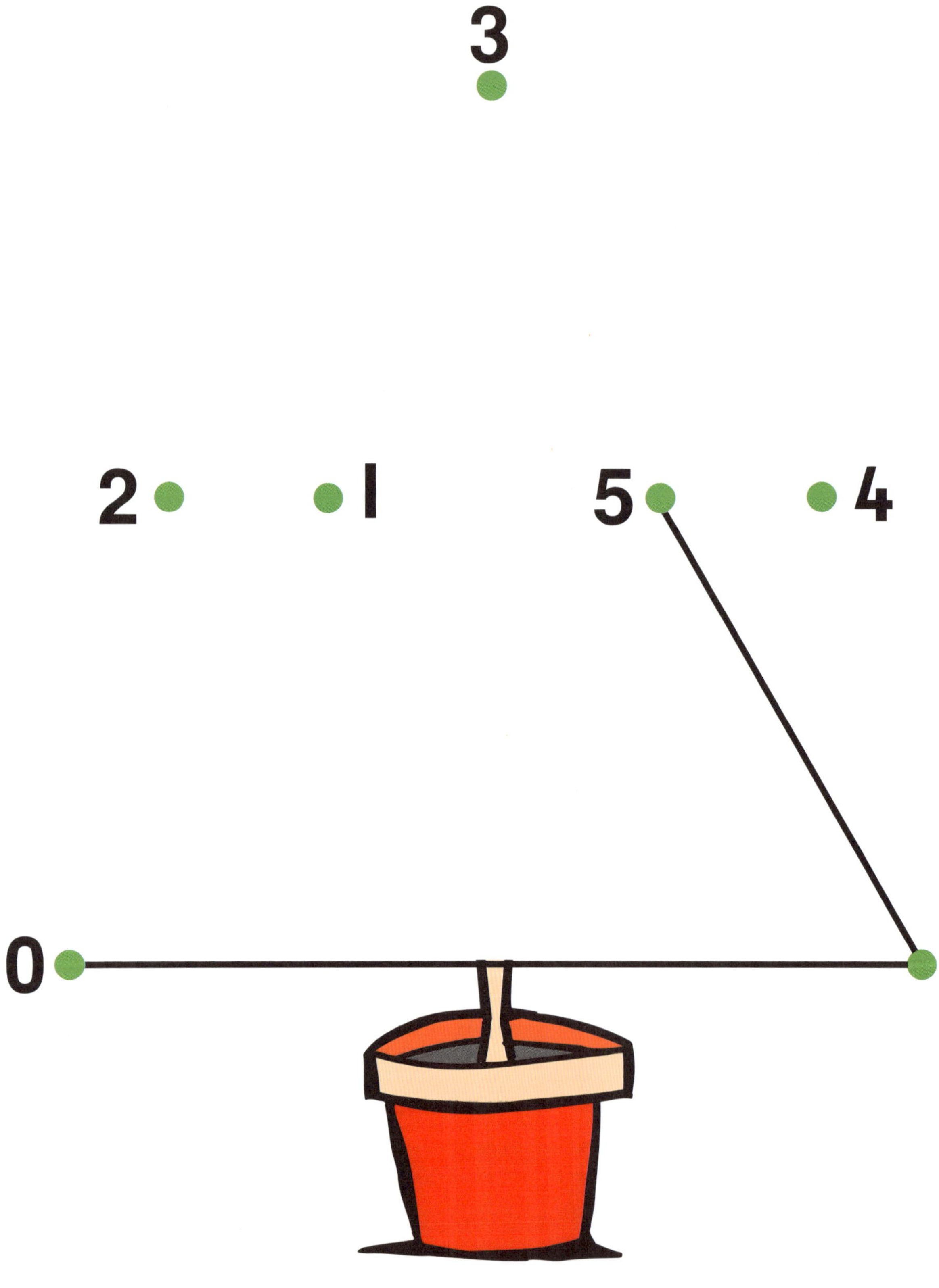

How many birds? ☐

How many starfish? ☐

How many balls? ☐

Count to 5

Count and colour the balls.

3

4

5

Learn to write the number 6

Follow the lines to write the number six.

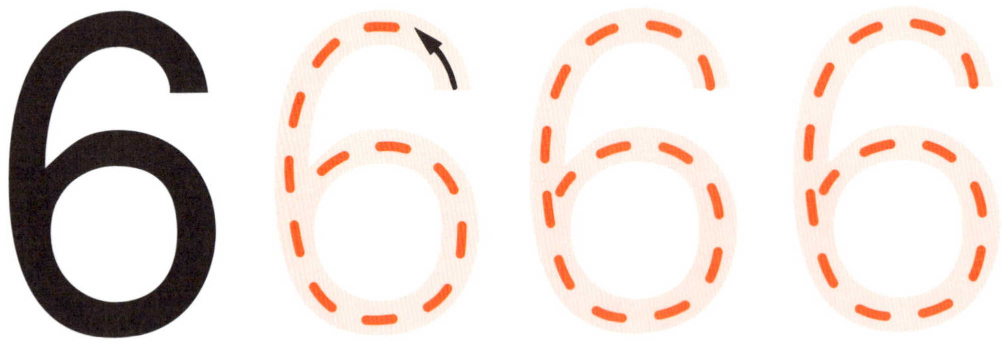

Count six hens.

Count six cups.
Colour six cakes.
How many saucers can you see?

How to practise counting skills

- **teach your child some well-known counting rhymes:**
e.g. 1, 2, 3, 4, 5 once I caught a fish alive, one man went to mow, ten green bottles, ten in the bed, etc.

- **show your child that you count yourself:**
e.g. when you pay for things at the shops.

- **make time for counting activities and games with your child:**
e.g. who can make a tower with the biggest number of bricks.

- **show your child that counting is fun,**
e.g. on long car journeys – you can pass the time by counting cars of different colours, or horses you spot in fields, etc.

Draw more pictures in each row to match the number six.

6 

6 

6 

6 

6 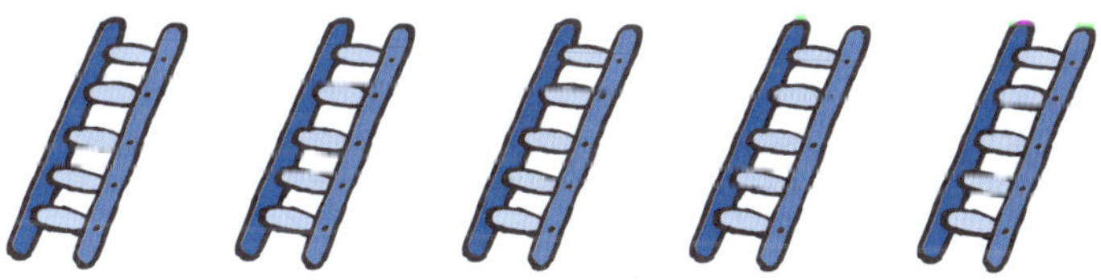

Count to 7

What can you see in the tree?
How many birds can you count?

How many birds in the tree now?
There are seven birds.

Learn to write the number 7

Follow the lines to write the number seven.

Count seven butterflies.

Count seven shells.
Colour seven fish.

Recognise numerals, count to 7

Count the fruit.
Draw lines to join the pictures to the numbers.

7

6

7

6

How many ants?
How many cakes?

Learn to write the number 8

Follow the lines to write the number eight.

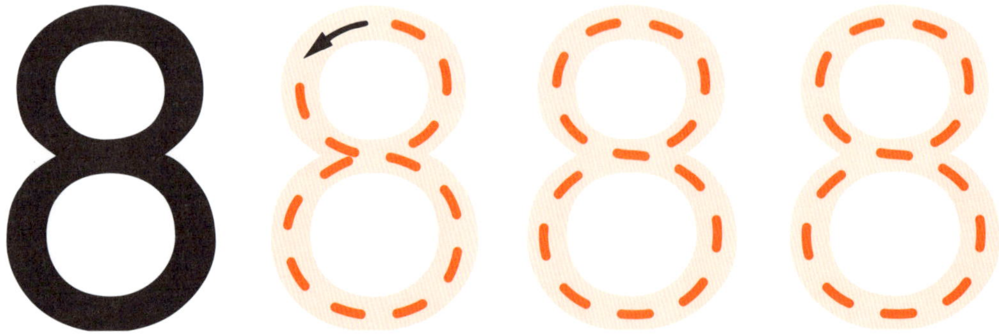

Count eight legs.

Count eight kites then colour them.

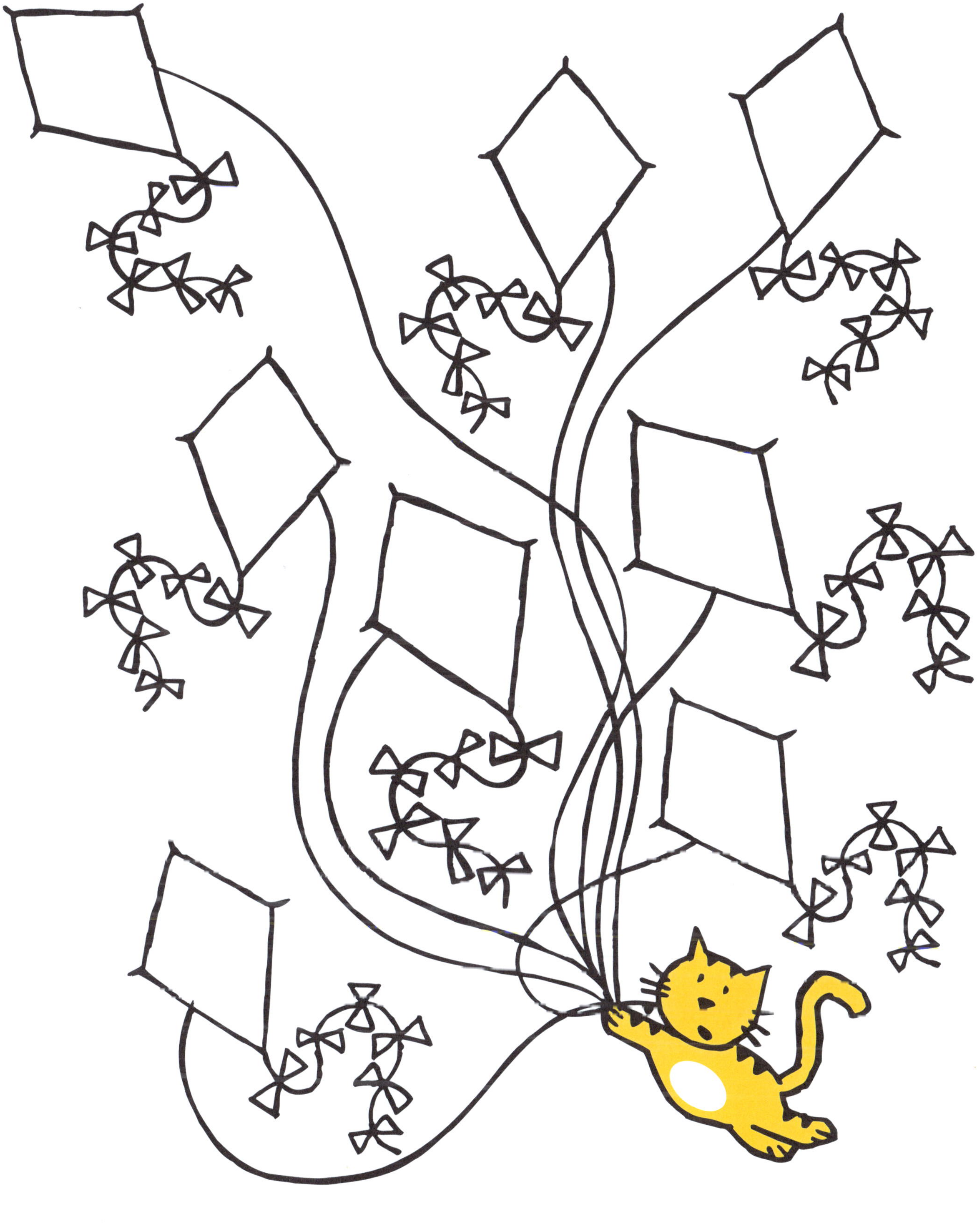

Recognise numerals, order numbers

Ring the numbers that match the pictures.

5 6 7 8

5 6 7 8

5 6 7 8

5 6 7 8

Say the door numbers in order.
Write the numbers on the doors.

Count to 8, recognise numerals

How many legs do spiders have?
Draw eight legs on the spider.

Ring the numbers that match the pictures.

6 7 8

6 7 8

6 7 8

6 7 8

Count to 9

How many birds are in this tree?
There are eight.

How many birds now?
What a lot of birds!
There are nine birds to count now.

Learn to write the number 9

Follow the lines to write the number nine.

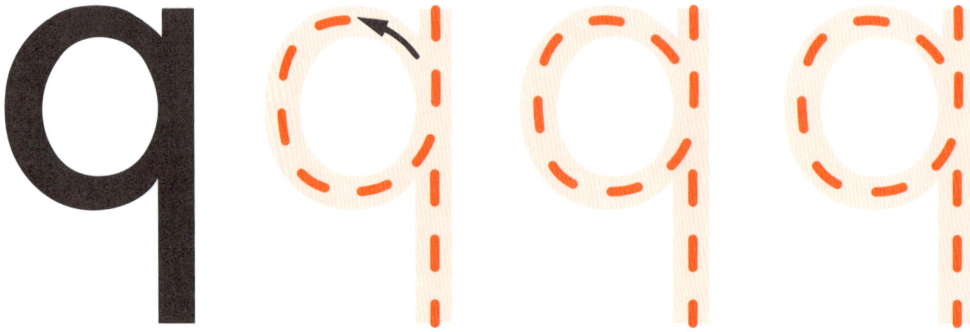

Count nine elephants.

Count nine flowers.
How many bees? Colour them.

Recognise numerals, count to 9

Count the dots.
Draw lines to join the dots to the numbers.

7

9

6

8

Count the bricks.
Write the number for each picture.

How many?

How many?

How many?

How many?

Addition to 9, count to 10

Draw more balls so that the clown has nine.

How many birds are in the tree now?

Learn to write the number 10

Follow the lines to write the number ten.

10

Count ten men.

Count ten birds.
Colour them.

Count to 10, recognise numerals

Ring the group of ten buttons.

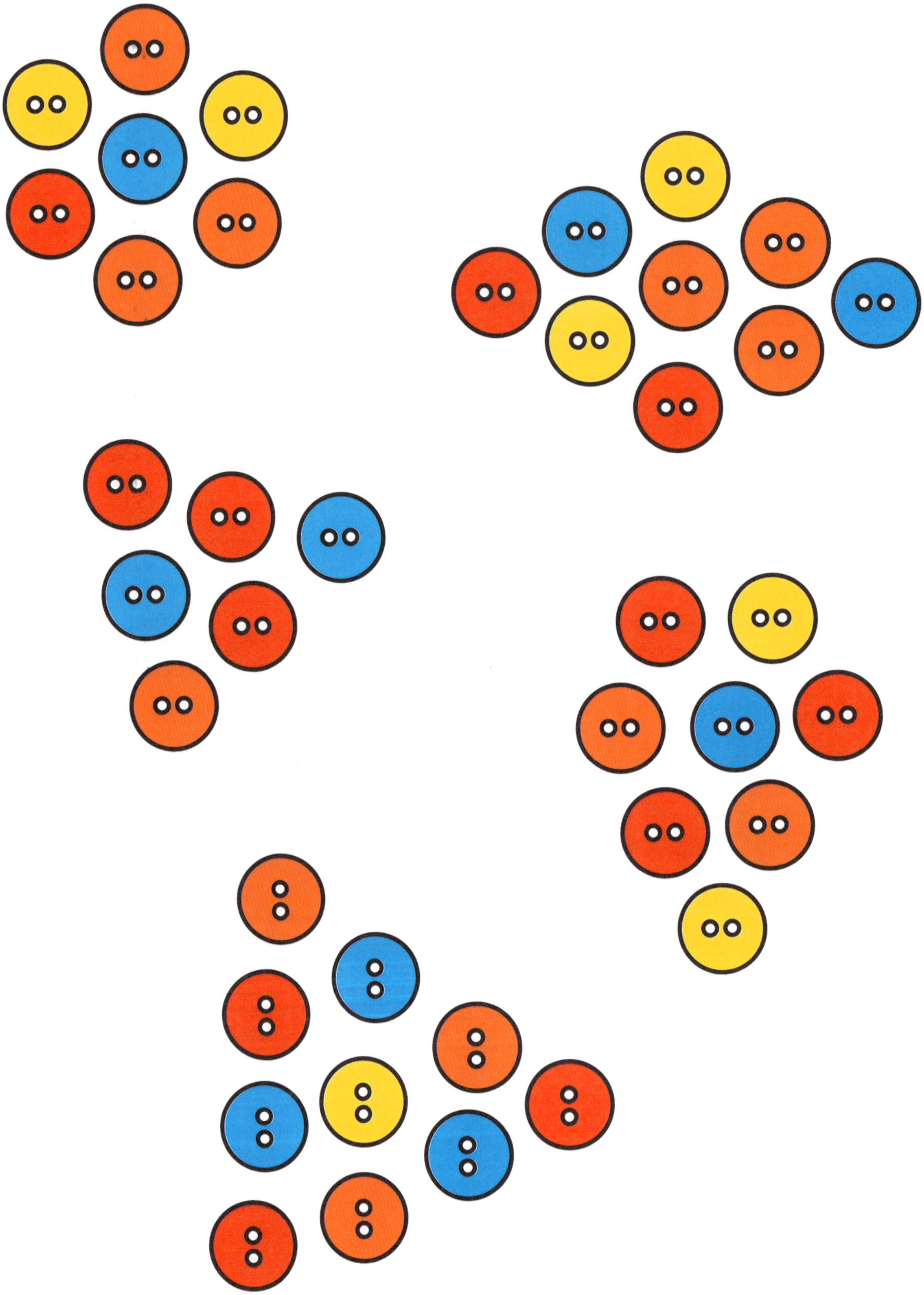

Ring the numbers that match the pictures.

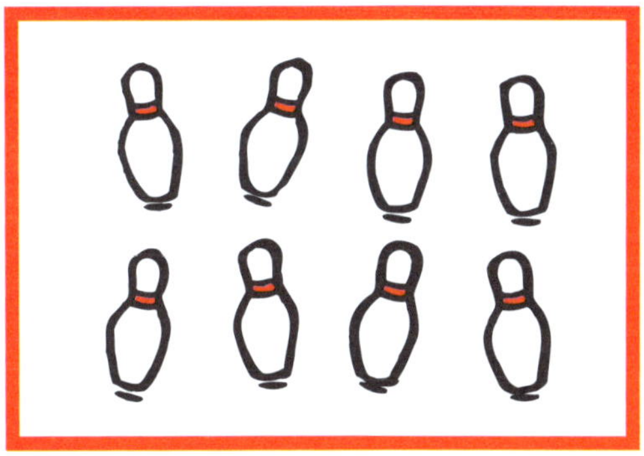

6 7 8 9 10

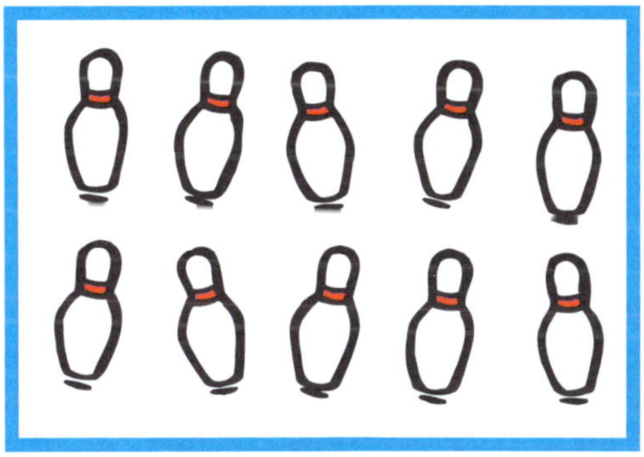

6 7 8 9 10

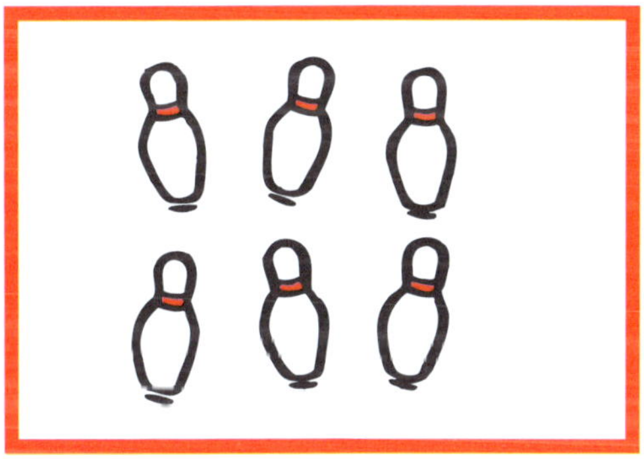

6 7 8 9 10

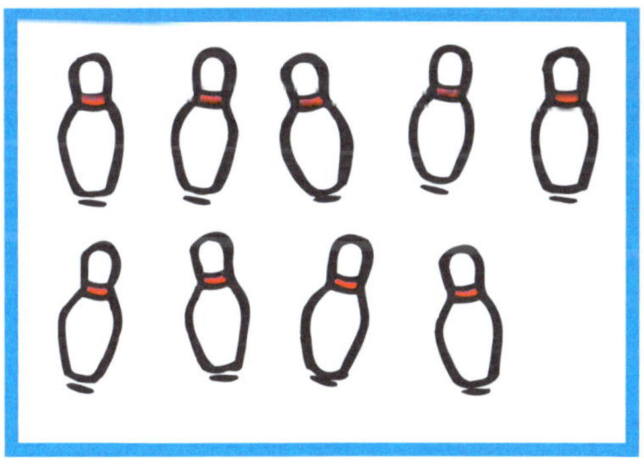

6 7 8 9 10

How to develop an understanding of numbers

Children have a natural curiosity about numbers and this needs to be encouraged in the following ways ...

- **talk about significant personal numbers:** e.g. your child's age or your house number.
- **explain how numbers are useful to us:** e.g. the numbers of the TV channels, bus numbers, car registration numbers.
- **find opportunities to use number language:** e.g. "how many altogether", "one more", "one less", "the number before", "the number after", etc.
- **compare numbers,** e.g. which number is larger?
- **talk about the names of very large numbers:** e.g. hundreds, thousands.

Say the car numbers in order.
Write the numbers on the cars.

Recognise numerals

Ring the group of ten triangles.

Draw lines to join the pictures to the numbers.

7

10

9

Order numbers

Put the numbers in the right order.
Draw them on the board.

6	10	9	7	8

Join the dots. Start at 0.
Count to 10.

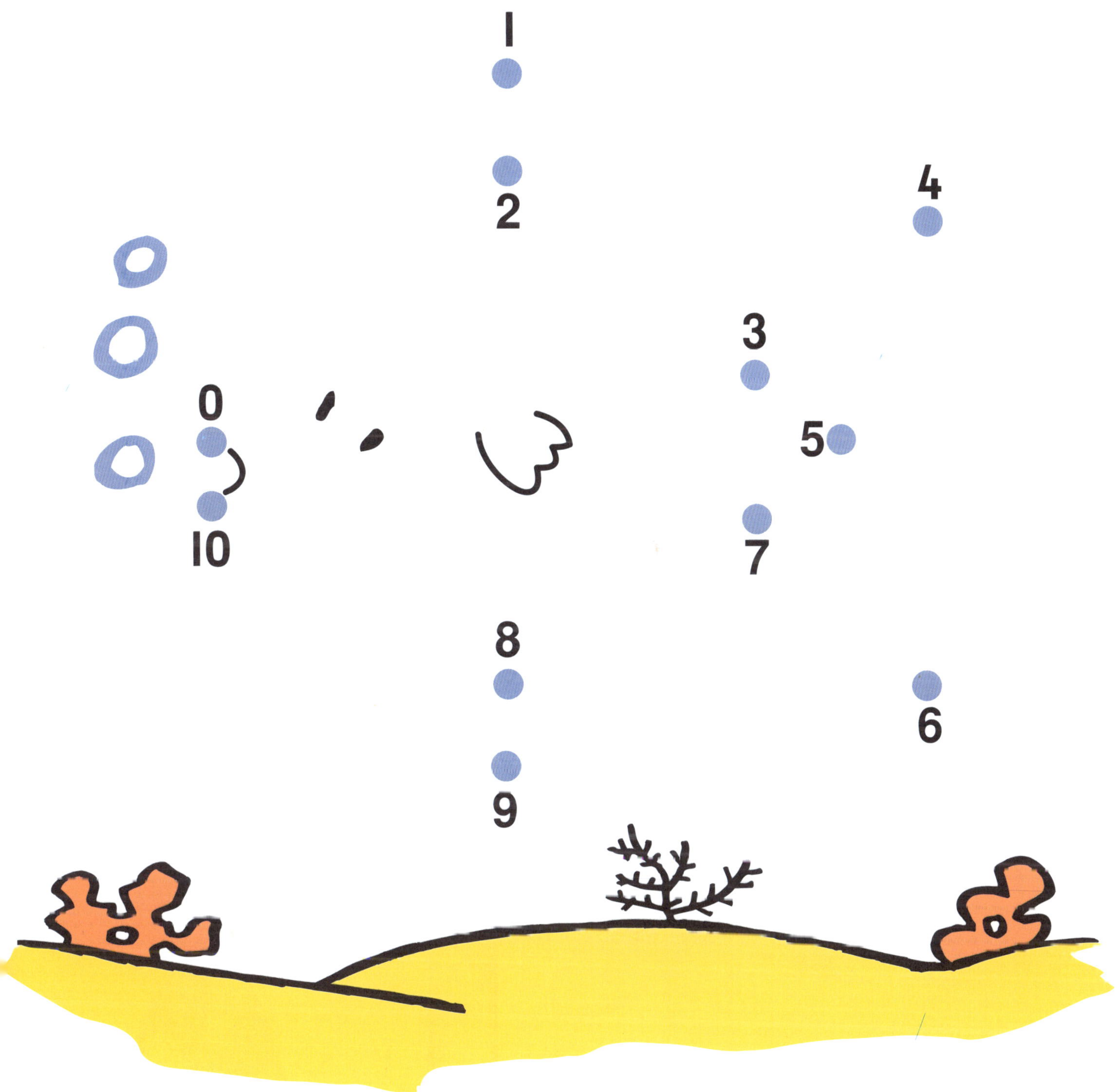

Addition to 10, recognise numerals

How many shoes?

How many socks?

Draw more socks to match the shoes.

Ring the numbers that match the pictures.

6 7 8 9 10

6 7 8 9 10

6 7 8 9 10

6 7 8 9 10

Addition to 10

Draw one more picture in each row.
Write how many altogether in each box.

Draw more shapes in each row.
The number of shapes must match the number in each box.

7	
10	
9	
6	
8	

Write numerals, count to 10

The clown has ten balls.
Write the numbers from one to ten on the balls.

Count the ladybirds in each group.
Write the number in each box.

☐ **ladybirds**

☐ **ladybirds**

☐ **ladybirds**

☐ **ladybirds**

Write numerals, addition to 10

There are ten steps to climb.
Write ten numbers, in order, on the steps.

Write numerals, addition to 10

Draw one more shape in each row.
Write how many altogether in each box.

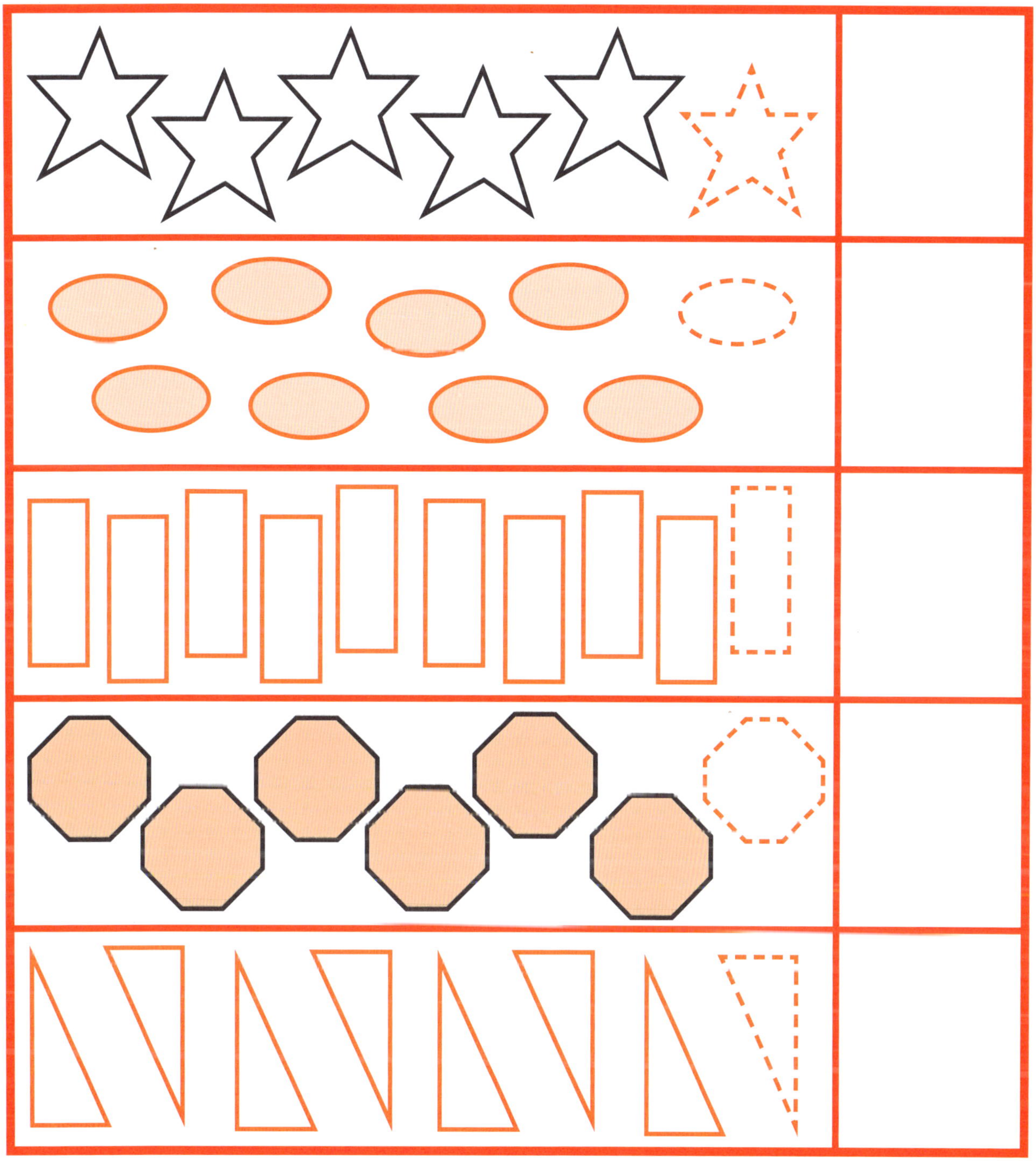

Learn to write the number 11

Follow the lines to write the number eleven.

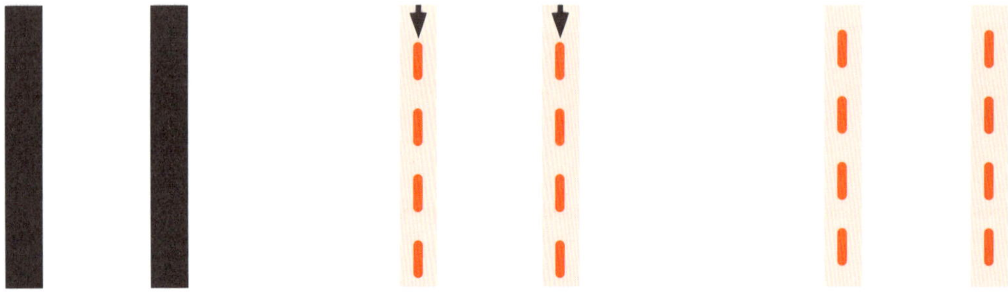

Count eleven footballers.

Colour eleven beads red.
Colour the others blue.

Write the numbers.

☐ **red beads** ☐ **blue beads**

Learn to write the number 12

Follow the lines to write the number twelve.

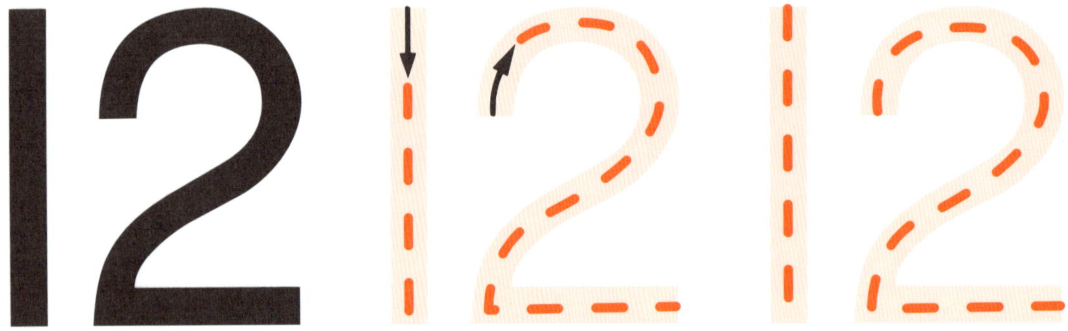

Count twelve bottles.

Colour ten cabbages.
Draw two more.

How many altogether?

☐ **cabbages**

Count to 12, addition to 12

Count 10 rabbits.
Draw two more rabbits.

How many altogether?

☐ **rabbits**

Draw more fish in the pond to make 12 altogether.
Count the trees.

☐ **trees**

Learn to write the number 13

Follow the lines to write the number thirteen.

13

Draw some more apples to make thirteen.

Colour thirteen bricks yellow.
Colour the others green.

Write the numbers.

☐ **yellow bricks** ☐ **green bricks**

Learn to write the number 14

Follow the lines to write the number fourteen.

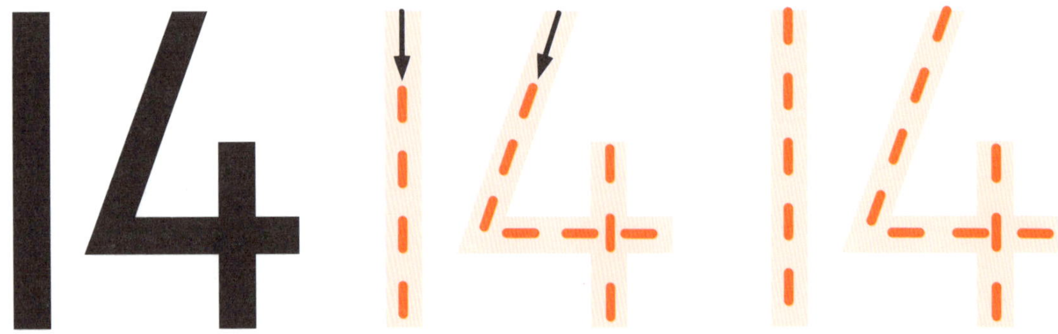

Count fourteen frogs.

Colour fourteen socks green.
Colour the others pink.

Write the numbers.

☐ **green socks** ☐ **pink socks**

Learn to write the number 15

Follow the lines to write the number fifteen.

15

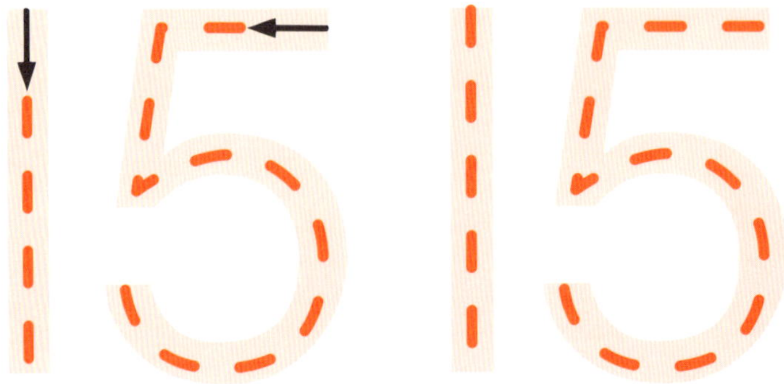

Count fifteen petals.

Colour ten squares.
Draw five more.

How many altogether?

☐ **squares**

Order numbers, addition to 15

Say the rocket numbers in order.

Write the numbers on the rockets.

Count 10 birds.
Draw 5 more birds.

How many altogether? ☐ **birds**

How to use numbers in practical ways

Everyday activities might involve:

- **setting the table at mealtimes for one more (addition) or for one less (subtraction), sharing biscuits or treats equally between children (division), estimating how many sandwiches to make for a party (multiplication).**
- **sorting and grouping objects,** *e.g. finding all the socks from the washing and then putting them into pairs.*
- **arranging objects in rows to help counting,** *e.g. eggs in egg boxes.*
- **"counting on" from a number rather than starting from one each time.**

Draw one egg for each chicken.
Count the eggs.

☐ **eggs**

Addition to 10, order numbers

Count the skittles.
Draw 5 more skittles.

How many altogether?

☐ **skittles**

The trains are in order.
Write in the missing number.

Write in the missing numbers on the trucks.

Learn to write the number 16

Follow the lines to write the number sixteen.

16 16 16

Count sixteen milk bottles.

Write 16, addition to 16

Colour ten triangles.
Draw six more.

How many altogether? ☐ **triangles**

Addition to 16, count to 16

Draw more shells to match the numbers.

12

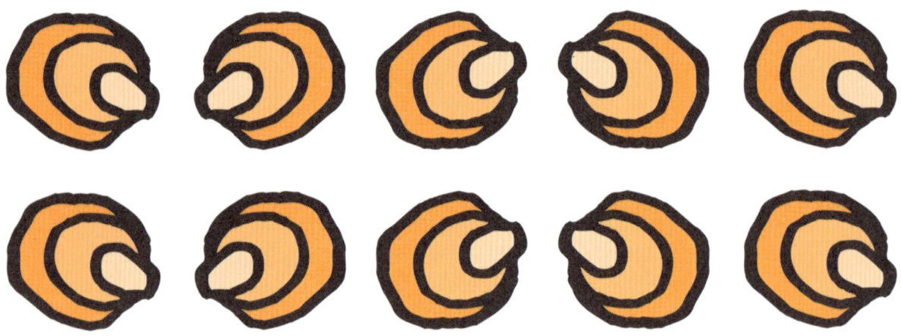

13

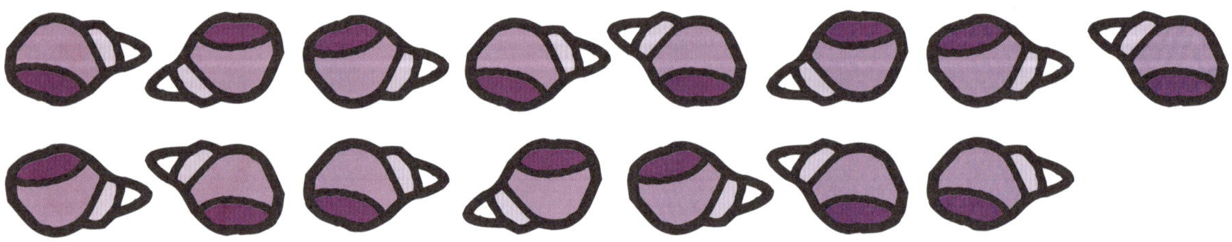

16

Count the triangles.

Count the squares.

Draw sixteen circles.

How many?

squares **triangles**

Learn to write the number 17

Follow the lines to write the number seventeen.

17 17 17

Count seventeen leaves.

Count the crocodile's teeth.
Draw some more teeth to make 17.

How many altogether?

☐ **teeth**

Learn to write the number 18

Follow the lines to write the number eighteen.

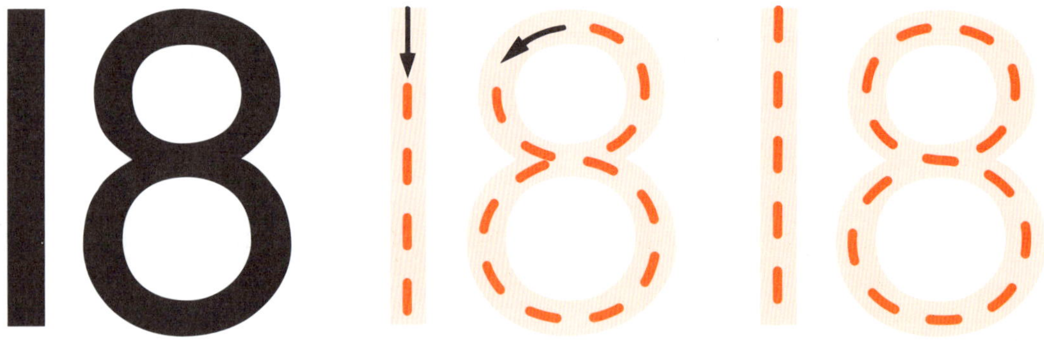

Count eighteen cars.

Colour the oranges.
Draw eight more oranges.

How many altogether?

☐ **oranges**

Addition to 18, count to 18

Count 13 shirts.
Draw 5 more shirts.

How many altogether? ☐ **shirts**

Count 10 sweets.
Draw 8 more sweets.

Count the pieces of chocolate. ☐ **pieces**

Learn to write the number 19

Follow the lines to write the number nineteen.

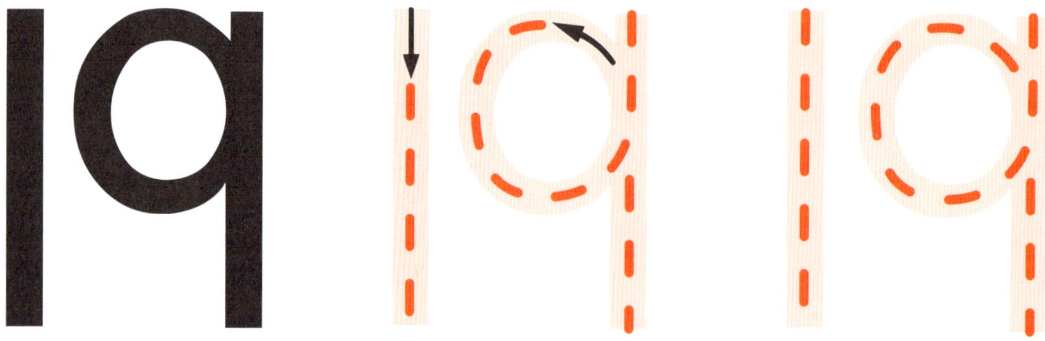

Count nineteen drums.

Colour nineteen trees green.
Colour any others brown.

Write the numbers.

☐ **green trees**

☐ **brown trees**

Learn to write the number 20

Follow the lines to write the number twenty.

Count twenty candles.

Colour ten buttons.
Draw ten more buttons.

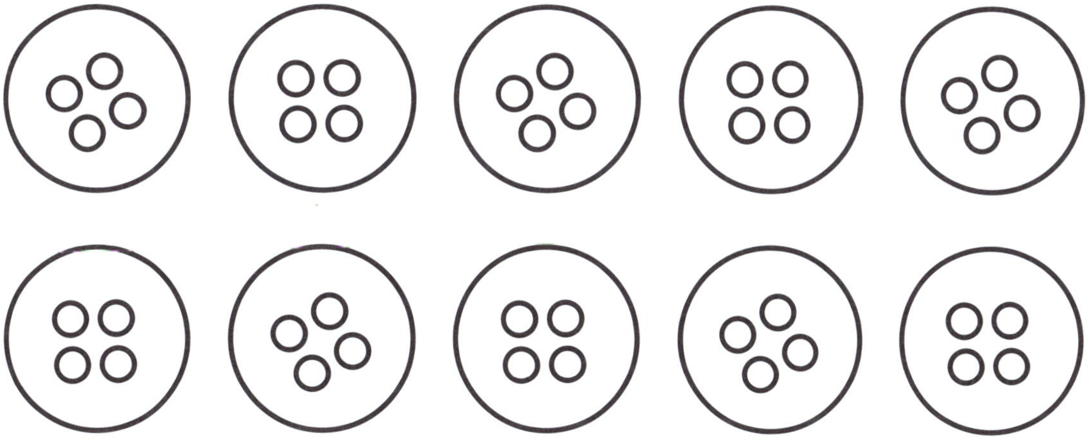

How many altogether?

☐ **buttons**

Order numbers, count to 20

Say the shirt numbers in order.
Write the numbers on the shirts.

Count 20 balloons.
Draw a cloud over one balloon.
How many can you see now?

Write the number.

☐ **balloons**

Recognise numerals, count in 2s

Ring the numbers that match the pictures.

16 17 18 19 20

16 17 18 19 20

16 17 18 19 20

16 17 18 19 20

Recognise numerals, count in 2s

Frog jumps along the path in twos.
Write the numbers the frog jumps on.

2	4								

Count in 3s, count in 4s

Kangaroo jumps along the path in threes.
Write the numbers the kangaroo jumps on.

3	6				

Count in 3s, count in 4s

Dinosaur jumps along the path in fours.
Write the numbers the dinosaur jumps on.

4				

zero
one
two
three
four
five
six
seven
eight
nine

ten
eleven
twelve
thirteen
fourteen
fifteen
sixteen
seventeen
eighteen
nineteen
twenty

count
match
altogether
number

Tick the boxes to show what you know!

Now I can ...

- [ ] count up to 5 objects
- [ ] count up to 10 objects
- [ ] count up to 15 objects
- [ ] count up to 20 objects
- [ ] point to the pictures, or objects, as I count
- [ ] say the numbers 0 to 10 in the correct order
- [ ] say the numbers 0 to 20 in the correct order
- [ ] write the numbers 0 to 10
- [ ] write the numbers 11 to 20
- [ ] match numbers to pictures
- [ ] add one more to a number
- [ ] add more to make a number
- [ ] recognise numbers 0 to 10
- [ ] recognise numbers 0 to 20

Look out for
the companion title:
Mega English 3–5

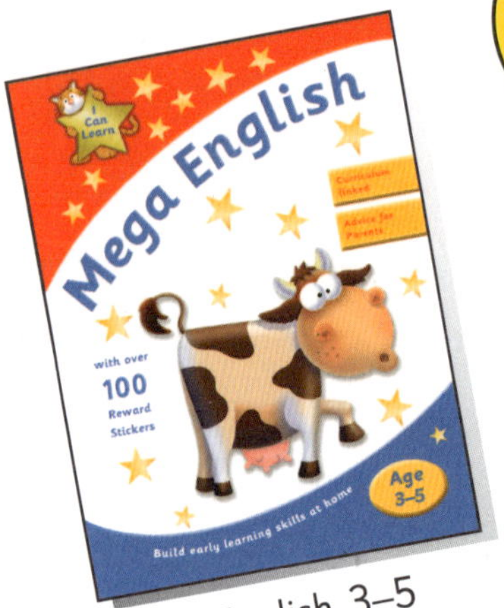

Mega English 3–5
ISBN 978 1 4052 4485 5

There are MEGA books for older children, too.

**Look out for Mega Maths 5–7
and Mega English 5–7.**

Mega Maths 5–7
ISBN 978 1 4052 4488 6

Mega English 5–7
ISBN 978 1 4052 4487 9

Each book is packed with 128 pages of learning exercises and 100 fun stickers to enjoy.

All titles comply with the National Curriculum (England and Wales) and English and Mathematics 5–14 (Scotland) and are in line with the Curriculum Guidance for the Foundation Stage, and the National Literacy and Numeracy Strategies.

These are the perfect books to help support your child's progress through primary school.